Charles,

    May you find an epic smash in each and every day.

    Thanks for all you do.

Dr. Mounce

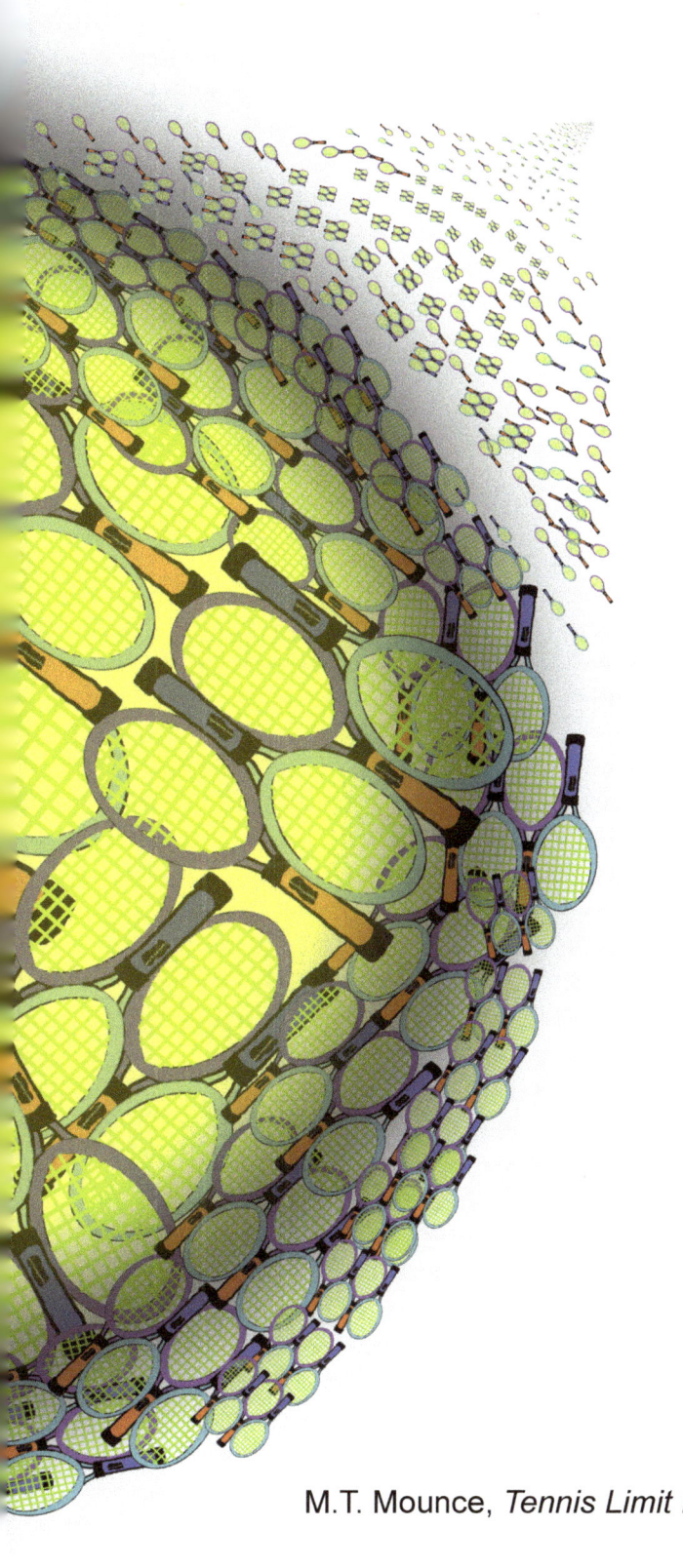

M.T. Mounce, *Tennis Limit I*, 2020.

To my inspirations.

Special thanks to CJ, Jennifer,
and Linda.

For D-Alli.

# Let's Play Tennis!

## A BABY BIGFOOT & BABY YETI Book
## By Dr. Mounce

Coma Toast Tacos    A Micropublisher

# The children are still asleep in their nests.

## Baby Bigfoot

ZZZZZZ z zZzzZz zZz z z z z z z z z

## Baby Giganto

# Baby Yeti

zZzZzZz zZzZZzZz z z z z z z

# Baby Sasquatch

# WHOO-OOP! Breakfast time!

Unnnn

Yes, Mama.

That was an ace.

SCORE! 200 to nothing!

Get ready for my new move, the mega-warrior!

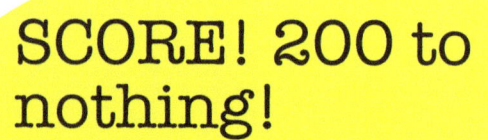

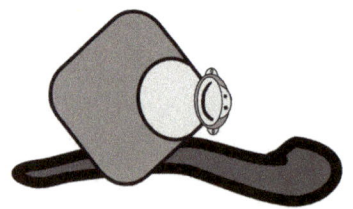

# ROAR!!

SWO

40 to 15.

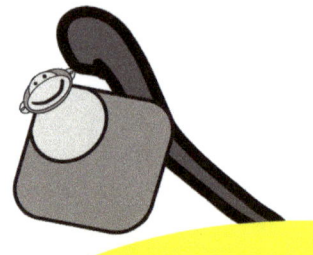

What time
is it?

CHQ

# GULP!

# THE

END

# Lunchtime.

Where are those avocados!?!?

**D**r. Mounce was born on Halloween in rural Pontotoc County, Mississippi. Following graduation from Ole Miss, he taught mathematics, physical education, health, adult education, and continuing education topics. During his tenure in Mississippi public schools, he also coached multiple sports, drove school bus routes, and taught night classes for a local college. Besides campaigns in basketball, tennis, baseball, and soccer, his coaching career included a golf State Championship. In 2006 he was invited to participate in the prestigious Mississippi State University Writing and Thinking Project. While there, he wrote the short story *Run For Your Life*, which was broadcast on Rural Voices Radio. He moved to North Carolina in 2010, where he rapidly ascended to associate professor on the collegiate level. His first book, *Squatching By Woods on a Snowy Evening*, is a highly acclaimed children's book about adventure and discovery. His hobbies include hiking, tennis, and sand volleyball. For more about Dr. Mounce, visit www.squatching.com, www.facebook.com/dr.mounce, https://www.instagram.com/dr.mounce, and https://twitter.com/drmounce1.

CPSIA information can be obtained
at www.ICGtesting.com
Printed in the USA
BVHW020512190520
579910BV00002BA/16